REFLECTIONS ON THE JOURNEY

A Ram Dass Inspired Journal

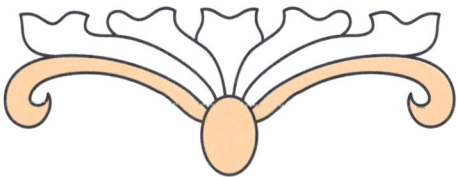

SAN RAFAEL LOS ANGELES LONDON

FOR RAM DASS
one who fervently embarked on the journey of life with rare openness, surrender and loving awareness.

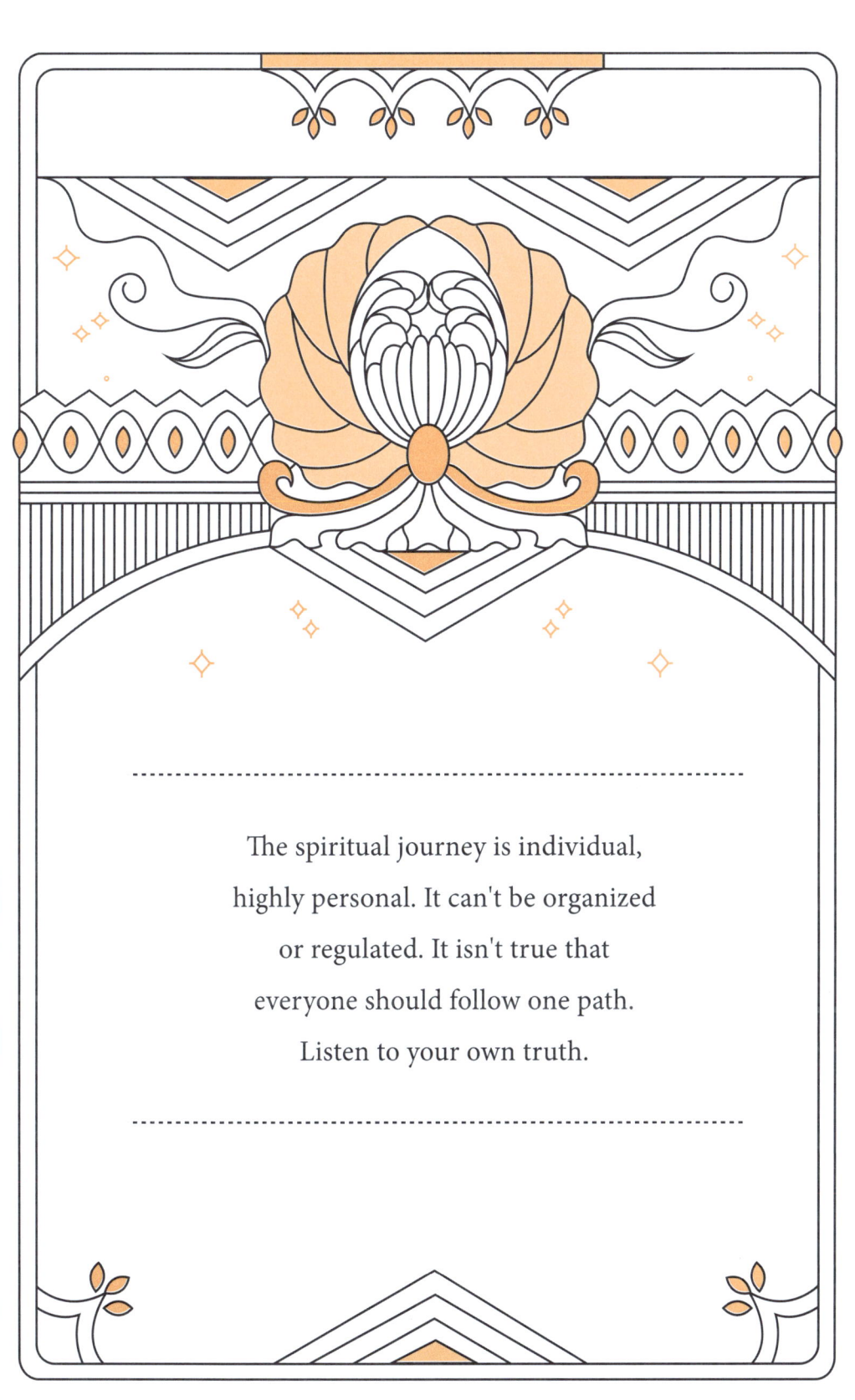

The spiritual journey is individual, highly personal. It can't be organized or regulated. It isn't true that everyone should follow one path. Listen to your own truth.

If you listen to your own inner voice
it will tell you where you are now and which
method will work best for you in your
evolution toward the light.

Trust the messages coming from your heart and intuition.

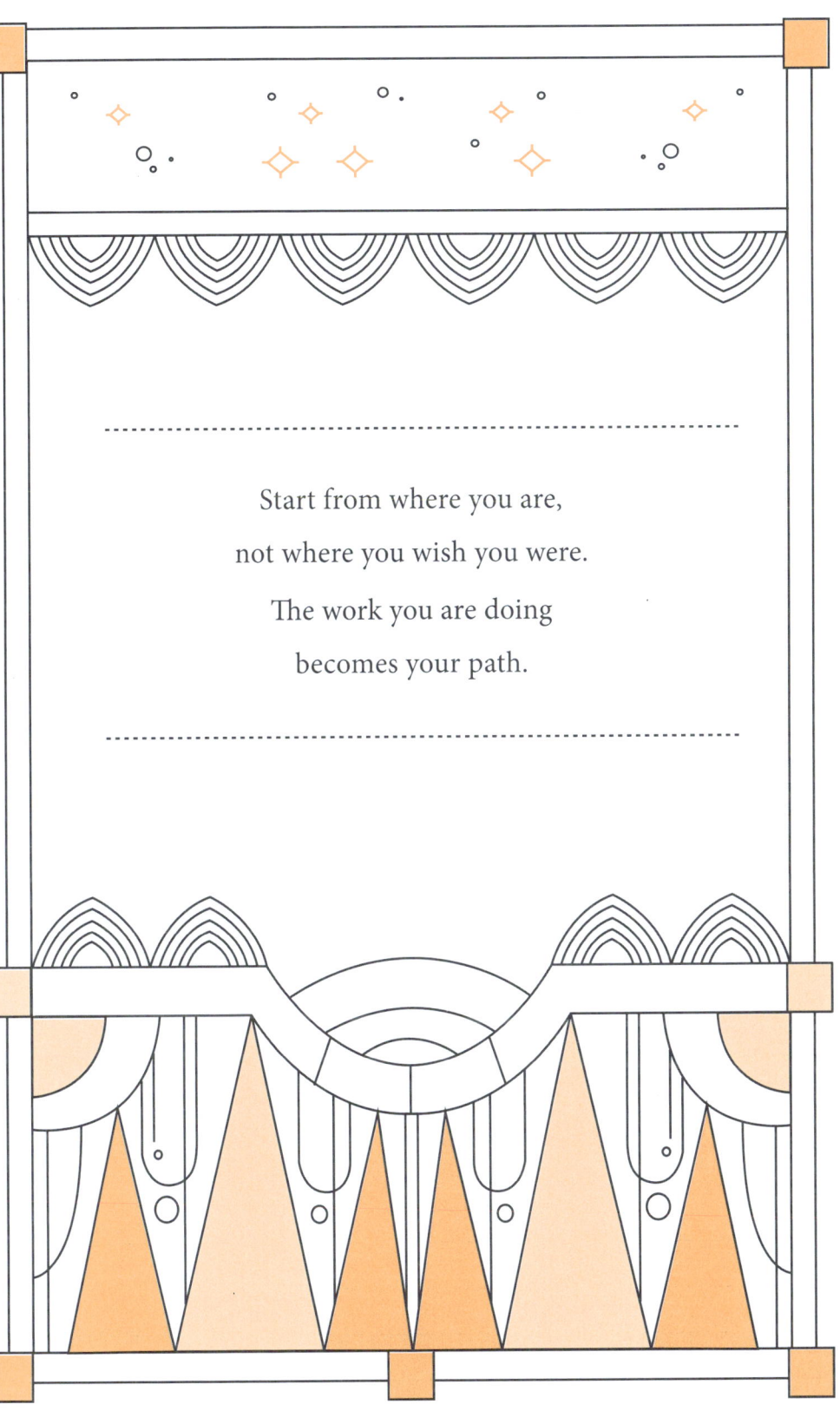

Start from where you are,
not where you wish you were.
The work you are doing
becomes your path.

It is important to expect nothing,

to take every experience,

including the negative ones,

as merely steps on the path,

and to proceed.

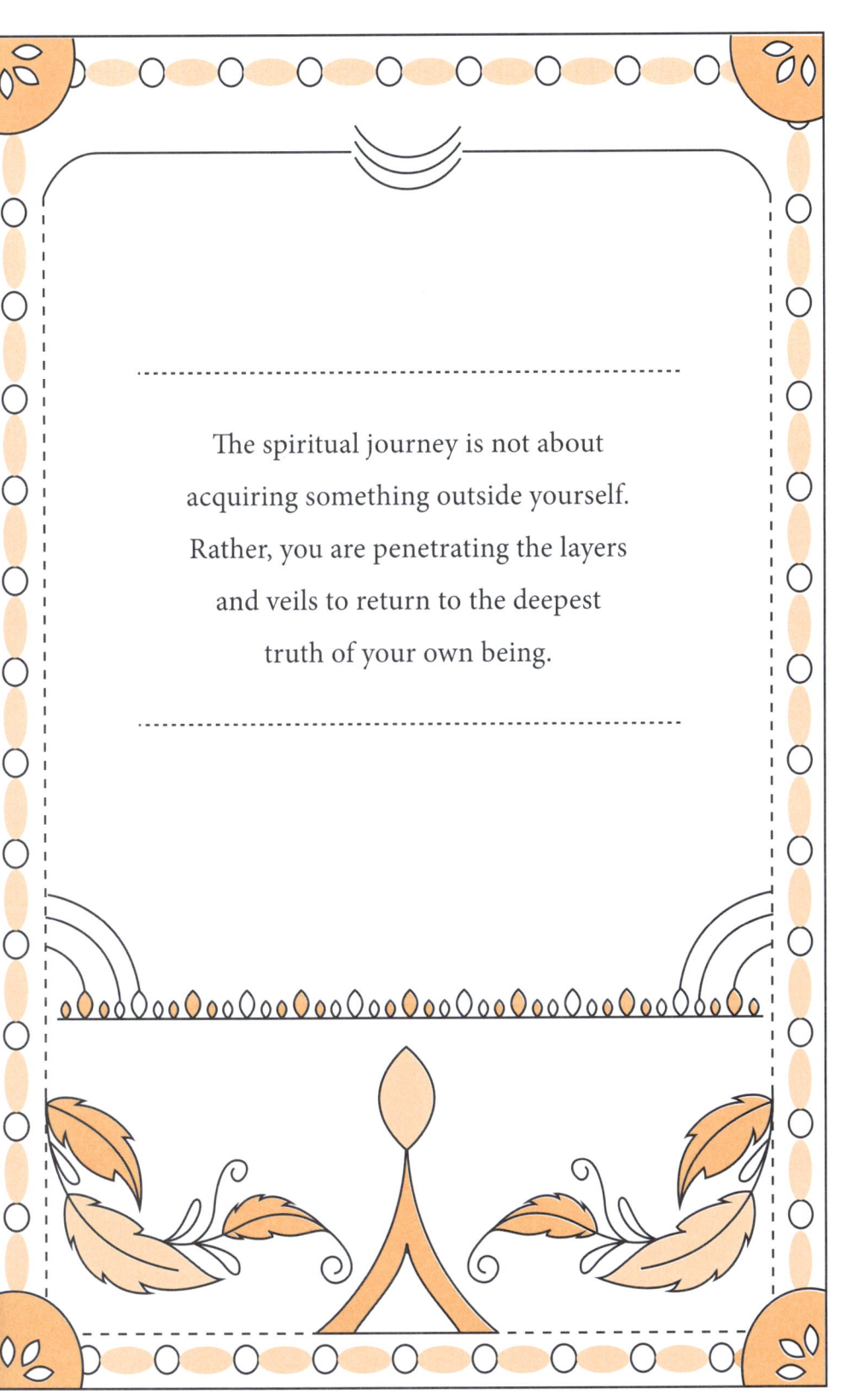

The spiritual journey is not about acquiring something outside yourself. Rather, you are penetrating the layers and veils to return to the deepest truth of your own being.

It's only when caterpillarness is
done that one becomes a butterfly.
That again is part of this paradox.
You cannot rip away caterpillarness.
The whole trip occurs in an unfolding
process of which we have no control.

Working on our own consciousness
is the most important thing
that we are doing at any moment.

The universe is made up of experiences that
are designed to burn out your attachment,
your clinging to pleasure, to pain, to fear,
to all of it. As long as there is a place
where you are vulnerable, the universe
will find a way to confront you with it.

As you quiet your mind,
you begin to see the nature
of your own resistance more clearly.
Struggles, inner dialogues, the way
in which you procrastinate and
develop passive resistance against life.
As you cultivate the witness, things change.
You don't have to change them.
Things just change.

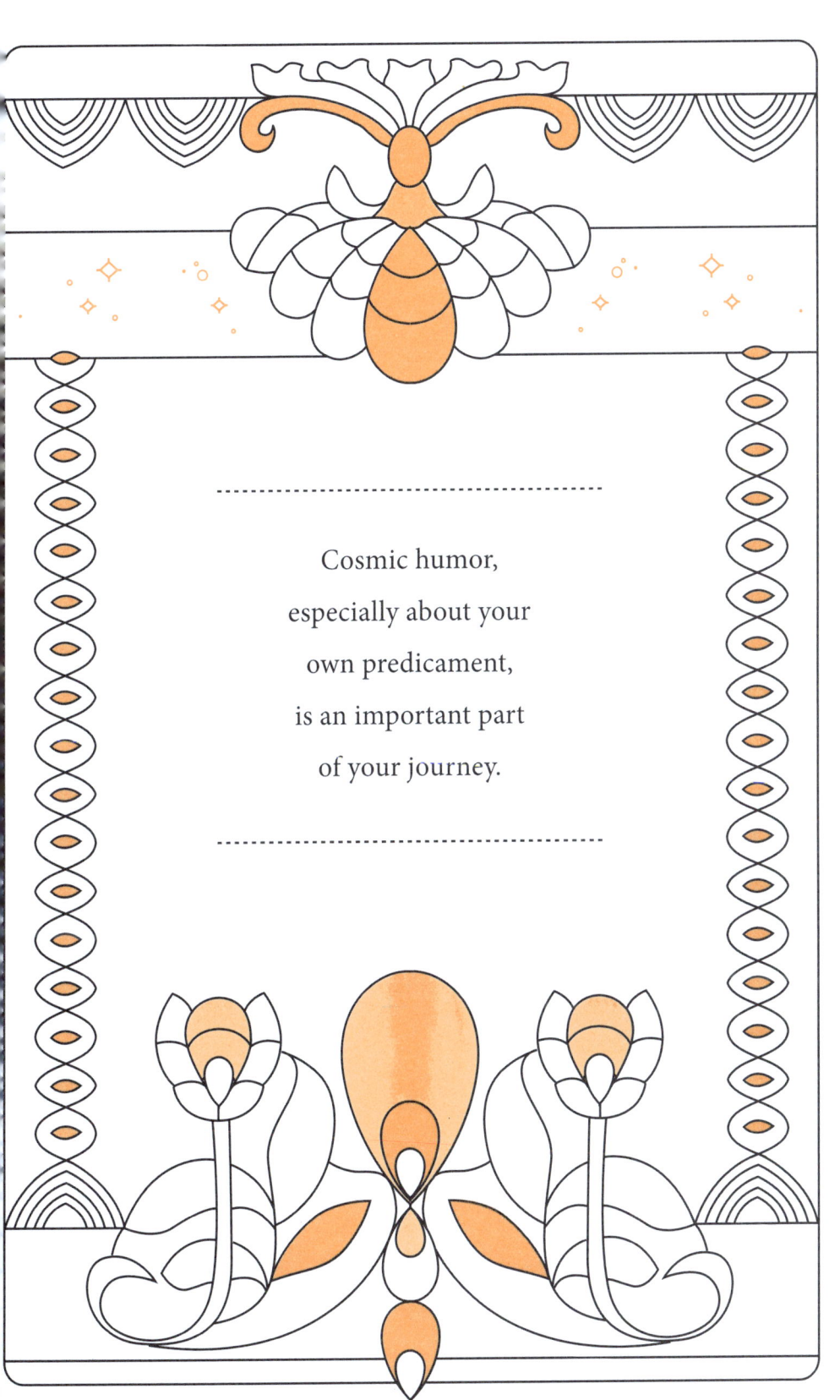

Cosmic humor, especially about your own predicament, is an important part of your journey.

Honoring Ram Dass into the
future and spreading his wisdom
to all seekers far and wide

© Jonathan Perugia / Gaia Visual

ABOUT RAM DASS

In 1967 Ram Dass was still Dr. Richard Alpert, a prominent Harvard psychologist and psychedelic pioneer with Dr. Timothy Leary. He continued his psychedelic research until he took a fateful trip to India later that year. In India, he met his guru, Neem Karoli Baba, who gave him the Hindu name Ram Dass, which means "servant of God." Everything changed then—his intense dharmic life started, and he became a pivotal influence on a culture that has reverberated with the words "Be Here Now" ever since. Ram Dass's spirit has been a guiding light for several generations.

From 1968 onward, Ram Dass pursued a panoramic array of spiritual methods and practices from ancient wisdom traditions including Buddhist meditation in the Theravadin, Mahayana Tibetan, and Zen Buddhist schools, and Sufi and Jewish mystical studies. He also practiced and taught bhakti yoga—which focuses on devotion and the Hindu deity Hanuman. Perhaps most significantly, his practice of karma yoga or spiritual service has opened up millions of other souls to their deep, yet individuated spiritual practice and path.

Ram Dass passed away at his home on Maui on December 22, 2019.

ABOUT THE
LOVE SERVE REMEMBER FOUNDATION

The Love Serve Remember Foundation is dedicated to preserving and continuing the teachings of Ram Dass and his guru Neem Karoli Baba. The foundation facilitates the continuation of these teachings through retreats, online courses and events, blog content, films, podcasts, social network channels and collaborative projects with conscious artists and musicians.

To find out more about Ram Dass and his teachings, visit
www.ramdass.org and beherenownetwork.com.